Book of Creatures

Art and Poetry by Countess Sica

A Book of Creatures

Art and Poetry Copyright © 2015 Countess Sica

Original Art Created with Colored Pencil

Cover Copyright © 2020

Creative Creature Publishing

All Rights Reserved.

No part of this book may be used or

reproduced in any manner whatsoever

without written permission from the

publishing company except for review purposes.

All inquiries should be made at

CreativeCreaturePublishing.com

Paperback ISBN: 978-0-9964983-5-7

For all the

Creatures out there

&

Monsters everywhere

Acknowledgments

Mary Shelley for Frankenstein's Monster
Washington Irving for the Headless Horseman
Lewis Carroll for the Jabberwocky
And all the stories, legends, myths, and lore
from which the creatures in this book originated.

A is for Alien
[ey-lee-*uh*n]

An inhabitant of a distant planet,

Who came from outer space.

With the pointed probes,

They choose to use

To greet the human race.

B is for Bigfoot
[big-*foo* t]

Over ten feet tall,

And covered with hair.

His name says it all.

He causes a scare,

Leaving footprints in forests

From here to there.

C is for Cyclops
[sahy-klops]

A simpleminded giant,

With a temper to terrify.

His sight is not reliant,

With only one eye.

If he is after you,

All you must do is hide.

D is for Dragon
[drag-*uh* n]

Fire breathing reptile,

With wings to take flight.

Thieving gold for his bed,

By plundering villages at night.

E is for Elf
[elf]

Some are helpful and kind,

Skilled in baking or shoe repair.

Others have devious minds,

Tricksters, scoundrels, and thieves,

Of these, you must beware.

F is for Frankenstein's Monster
[frang-k*uh* n-stahyn s] [mon-ster]

A lonely doctor's creation,

Made from dead men's spare parts.

Brought back with electricity,

A jolt to the heart.

Large, scared, and clumsy,

He is a frightening sight.

Fear causes villagers' torches to light.

G is for Gargoyle
[gahr-goil]

Stone carved,

Upon the top of a church.

Protecting, or warning,

From his perch.

H is for Headless Horseman
[hed-lis]　　　[hawrs-m*uh* n]

A man without his head,

Uses a pumpkin instead.

When he rides his dark steed,

It is time to take heed.

I is for Imp
[imp]

A devilish minion,

With flesh, vibrant red.

Bright yellow eyes

Appear under your bed.

J is for Jabberwocky
[jab-er-wok-ee]

With vibrant scales and

Colored feathers,

A creature born from imagination.

Biting jaws and slashing claws,

She causes much vexation.

K is for Kraken
[krah-k*uh* n]

With barbed tentacles,

And snapping jaws,

He terrorized the sea.

Drowning sailors,

With his giant claws,

Leaving ocean debris.

L is for Lycanthrope
[lahy-kan-throhp]

A werewolf with a vicious bite.

Turns man to beast

In the full moon's light.

Snarling and growling,

A most fearful sight.

A silver weapon

Will end his plight.

M is for Mummy
[muhm-ee]

Raised from the dead,

Revenge, his determination.

Conjuring sandstorms,

And beetle swarms,

Brings his enemies to elimination.

N is for Nymph
[nimf]

Wingless fairy of nature,

Helping plants to grow.

With powerful magic,

For which they bestow.

O is for Ogre
[oh-ger]

A beastly thing,

Ugly and mean.

With a taste for flesh

And a nasty scream.

Swearing and shouting,

He is quite obscene.

P is for Person
[pur-s*uh* n]

A tasty morsel,

Delicious treat,

Which other creatures

Try to eat.

Q is for Quinotaur
[kwin-noh-tar]

A five-horned beast,

Which lives in the sea.

With a bull's head and fish tail,

It is as strange as can be.

R is for Reaper
[ree-per]

Collector of the dead,

Who comes for your soul.

Insights fear and dread

Beyond your control.

S is for Siren
[sahy-r*uh*n]

She sings most appealing,

Her enchantment is reeling.

It is strange you'll be feeling,

When your soul, she is stealing.

T is for Troll
[trohl]

Can't pass his bridge

Unless permitted.

A riddle to solve,

You must be quick-witted.

Stinking,

Belches and farts emitted.

U is for Unicorn
[yoo-ni-kawrn]

Pointed magical horn of gold,

Pure of heart, a gentle soul.

A beautiful beast to behold.

Enchanted forests, it does patrol.

V is for Vampire
[vam-pahy*uh* r]

Hypnotizing eyes,

You'll believe all his lies.

In sunlight he fries.

It is at night he flies.

A stake through the heart

Will be his demise.

W is for Witch
[wich]

Mixing potions, cursing brew,

Casting spells, a hex on you.

Cackling wildly under the moon,

While flying upon her magic broom.

These are the things that witches do.

X is for Xexeu
[zoo-zoo]

This is a bird,

Great in the sky.

Bringer of thunder,

And rain to the dry.

Y is for Yeti
[yet-ee]

Abominable Snowman,

He is also known.

With a terrible temper,

Best leave him alone.

Z is for Zombie
[zom-bee]

Once a person,

Not dead or alive.

Eating brains

Is how they thrive.

Keep a machete handy

If you want to survive.

www.ingramcontent.com/pod-product-compliance
Lightning Source LLC
Chambersburg PA
CBHW041950110426
42744CB00026B/8